The Tale of Tales

The Tale of Tales

Tony Mitton

Illustrated by Peter Bailey

PICTURE CORGI

THE TALE OF TALES
A PICTURE CORGI BOOK 978 0 552 54887 8

First published in Great Britain by David Fickling Books
an imprint of Random House Children's Books

David Fickling Books edition published 2003
Picture Corgi edition published 2007

1 3 5 7 9 10 8 6 4 2

Picture Corgi Books are published by Random House Children's Books,
61–63 Uxbridge Road, London W5 5SA,
a division of The Random House Group Ltd,
in Australia by Random House Australia (Pty) Ltd,
20 Alfred Street, Milsons Point, Sydney, NSW 2061, Australia,
in New Zealand by Random House New Zealand Ltd,
18 Poland Road, Glenfield, Auckland 10, New Zealand,
in South Africa by Random House (Pty) Ltd,
Isle of Houghton, Corner Boundary Road & Carse O'Gowrie,
Houghton 2198, South Africa, and in India by
Random House India PVT Ltd, 301 World Trade Tower,
Hotel Intercontinental Grand Complex, Barakhamba Lane,
New Delhi 110001, India

THE RANDOM HOUSE GROUP Limited Reg. No. 954009
www.kidsatrandomhouse.co.uk

A CIP catalogue record for this book is available from the British Library.

Printed in Singapore

Once upon a time, in a jungle far, far away, a bright new day was just beginning. As the sun came up, steam rose in wisps from the treetops. The air was full of the shrieks and calls of the animals, and the cries of the birds. It was a morning like so many mornings in the jungle. But this morning was special. For it was the morning of The Tale of Tales, and of the Story Road that led to it. And it is just at this moment that our story begins, with one particular monkey.

Come. Come closer and listen.

Monkey stretched and yawned. He picked a flea or two out of his hairy belly, scratched himself all over and climbed

nimbly up the mango tree to get his breakfast. He was just reaching out for a plump, ripe fruit, when he heard the sound of voices floating down from above. Squawky voices.

"Hmm. Parrots," he thought to himself. "I wonder what the gossip's about."

So up he went to sneak a listen. The voice was speaking slowly and strongly, pausing for effect once the words were spoken,

"And they do say it's to be the greatest story ever, The Tale of Tales . . ."

"Well," replied the other. "It's only a short flight from here to Volcano Valley, for those of us with wings. Let's make a day of it. Let's preen our fine feathers and fly off to hear this Tale of Tales. I can hardly wait. I wonder what it'll be about?"

"Me too," said the first. "Tell you what

though. Let's keep this to ourselves. We don't want too many ground animals turning up. They're so noisy and they take up too much room. Let's keep this for the birds. We'll get to hear better that way."

That was as much as Monkey needed to hear. Curious and eager as ever, he was down that tree in no time, and working out the easiest and quickest route to Volcano Valley.

"Wow!" he chattered to himself. "I've just got to hear that. The Tale of Tales!" And he set off at once through the jungle.

Whack! At the first bend in the trail he walked slap into Elephant who was coming the other way.

"Steady," rumbled Elephant. "Steady, old friend. What's the rush so early in

the morning?" Gently, he used his trunk to lift Monkey to his feet and dust him off.

"It's the greatest story ever, The Tale of Tales!" gibbered Monkey.

"Where?" said Elephant, looking around as if he expected to see it hovering nearby in the jungle.

"Volcano Valley. Later today. I heard two parrots squawking about it up the mango tree just now. They weren't going to tell us. But I'm going to hear it anyway. I'm not missing that for anything. Are you coming? Go on. Think of it. The Tale of Tales."

"Well, I do like a good story," said Elephant thoughtfully. "And it is very tempting, if it really is the greatest ever. I suppose there's only one way to find out."

"Yes," said Monkey scrambling up to sit on Elephant's neck. "And if I sit up here we can chat as we go

"Well, I do like a good story," said Elephant thoughtfully.

along. Come to think of it, I could tell you a story of my own. That would pass the time nicely."

"Alright," said Elephant. "What's it to be?"

Monkey thought for a moment. Then he spoke.

"This one's an old favourite of mine. It's about a very clever servant girl."

So the two companions made their way along the cool, green jungle trail, as Monkey sat on Elephant's neck and recited the tale of The Clever Servant.

The Clever Servant

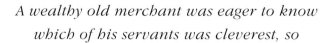

A wealthy old merchant was eager to know
which of his servants was cleverest, so

he called them together in order to ask
each of the trio to tackle a task.

'What you must do is to fill up my store
as much as you can, and, if possible, more!

'But here is the catch, as I'm sure you'll agree:
to do it you'll only have one rupee . . .'

The first took his money and set out to try
for something incredibly cheap he could buy.

He passed by a labourer deep in a dig.
'Ah,' thought the servant, 'a pile of earth's big.

'I can get masses for one rupee's worth.
This is the answer: a large mound of earth.'

So, swiftly he bought it and took it to town:
a mound of moist soil, so earthy and brown.

The merchant said, 'Good . . .' as he sized up the load.
'But look, it's your fellow, out there on the road.'

And up came the second with a cartload of straw.
Although not as heavy, its fullness seemed more.

It glimmered so goldenly, there in its pile,
that the merchant said, 'Clever!'
and gave a broad smile.

Then they sat and they waited for young number three,
to find what her answer would turn out to be.

At last she appeared. The merchant said, 'So.
Where is your purchase? Nothing to show?'

The servant stayed silent, but held out her hand.
'What!?' cried the merchant. 'I don't understand.

'This is a candle. It's ever so small.
A candle like this can fill no space at all.'

 'Come,' said the servant, and entered the room.
The others all followed and stood in the gloom.

The girl lit the candle and soon it shone bright.
'See, now,' she whispered: 'a roomful of light.

'Light that your scales cannot measure or hold.
But filling the darkness with glorious gold.'

'Ah!' gasped the merchant. 'Then this takes the prize.
I thought to test you. But you've opened my eyes.'

'See, now,' she whispered: *'a roomful of light.'*

"What a wise and wonderful story," said Elephant. "I must try to remember it."

"I thought elephants remembered everything," replied Monkey. "Don't they?"

"Yes, but I mean especially," murmured Elephant. "The thought of that lovely golden light . . . Ooof!"

Elephant stopped. A very large boulder lay right in his path,

blocking the trail. It must have rolled down from the hillside and lodged there.

"We can't have that," said Elephant. And with his great strength he groaned and pushed until he'd rolled the boulder off the path and into the undergrowth. Monkey looked down from above and marvelled at his friend's great strength. It wasn't long before they were off along the trail again, great big lolloping Elephant and little Monkey, sitting neatly up on his neck.

"Actually, that reminds me of a tale I could tell you," said Elephant thoughtfully. "It's a story my father used to tell me

when I was little. And it's all about people and how clever they are
. . . or not," he added with a chuckle.

"Go on, then. Tell it, tell it," said Monkey eagerly. And as
Elephant began, he sat quietly picking fleas from his fur and
flicking them away with his nimble fingers while he listened.

The Obstacle

Five men found their pathway blocked.
Something was in their way.
The night was dark, so what it was
they couldn't surely say.

Said the first,
stroking the shape,
'There's no mistake.
It's surely a kind of snake.'

Said the second,
touching the tip
of something sharp,
'No. It would appear
it's a sword or a spear.'

Said the third,
feeling about,
'I'm hotter. You're colder.
I could be sure
it's more . . . like a boulder!'

'According to me,'
said the fourth,
down on one knee,
'it resembles the trunk of a tree.'

'I can't agree,'
said the fifth,
as a bit of it
flicked in his eyes.
'I'd say it's a swarm of flies.'

Then off those five men wandered,
pondering busily whether
all of these separate facts
could be fitted together,

leaving the creature
to smile to itself in the night
at the thought of them being so wrong
(while a little bit right).

For the snake
was its trunk.
And the point
was its tusk.
And the boulder, that
was its bulk so thick.
And the trunk of the tree,
why, that was its knee.
And the flies . . .
were its tail
going flick, flick, flick.

leaving the creature to smile to itself in the night

"Oh . . ." said Monkey, looking puzzled. "So what was it, exactly? Some kind of spooky monster?"

"No, don't you see?" said Elephant with exasperation. But just then they were interrupted by a loud bleat that came from the slope above them.

"Maaaaaah! Hey, fellers!" They turned to see Goat, chomping greedily at a clump of fresh grass.

"Where are you off to?" she gulped.

"We are off," said Monkey importantly, "to hear The Tale of Tales. Down at Volcano Valley. Late this afternoon."

"We hope," added Elephant.

"And we're telling stories as we go," said Monkey. "For company and to pass the time. Would you like to come along?"

"Well, this grass is nearly all finished now," chewed Goat. "And I like a good story. And it's a nice day. So why not? OK. Count me in." And she trotted down to join them on the path.

"So do you know a good story you could tell us?" asked Elephant politely, as they began to wander down the trail together.

"I know a thousand and one," boasted Goat. "But the biggest and the best is the tale of The Bag. Though let me warn you. It's a bit hard to swallow."

So with Elephant tromping and Goat trotting and Monkey perched neatly up on Elephant's neck, the three companions made their way along the Story Road to the sound of Goat's bleaty voice reciting the old Arabian tale.

The Bag

Ali had been to the market.
He'd wanted some shopping from there:
Some bread and some dates, some fine
wooden plates,
and a wonderful turban to wear.

The turban he used as a basket
to carry his load of sweet dates.
He balanced the bread on the top of his head,
but he just kept on dropping the plates.

Said Ali, 'I wish I had something
to carry these tricky things in.'
Then suddenly, out, with a whoosh and a shout,
from the turban there tumbled a djinn!

from the turban there tumbled a djinn!

Well, a djinn is a kind of a genie
who can magic a wish to come true.
And I shouldn't suppose that there's
anyone knows
of a thing that a djinn cannot do.

So Ali thought, 'This could be useful.
A djinn is not easy to find.
Since I need a basket, I could try and ask it.
I'm sure that the djinn wouldn't mind.'

'Oh, djinn, can you spell me a holdall
to carry my shopping for me,
a bag sort of hollow that's able to swallow
whatever it happens to be?'

The djinn gave a whirl and a crackle
and melted back into the air.
But down on the track, looking simple and black,
a shopping bag came to be there.

Well, Ali got loading his shopping.
But what do you think that he found?
It gobbled it in with a kind of a grin
and then made a gurgling sound.

Ali was simply delighted,
and he set off again on his way.
His bag felt so light and the sun shone so bright –
in short, what a wonderful day!

But, just as he skipped round a corner,
in the dust of the roadway there stood
a horrible thug with a big ugly mug
and a knobbly cudgel of wood.

'Hand over your bag or I'll clonk you,'
the horrible robber then said.
With a terrible sneer he sidled up near
with his club in the air by his head.

He reached his hand out to the djinn-bag.
And, although it looked simple and small,
the bag gave a frown and gobbled him down,
ugly mug, cudgel and all.

Ali was simply astonished,
but the bag felt as light as a feather.
So he went on his way in the heat of the day,
enjoying the very fine weather.

All of a sudden two soldiers
came galloping up in a sweat.
'A thief's robbed the King of his favourite ring
and we're hunting that robber, you bet!

'So give us that bag that you've got there,
for everyone has to be searched.'
As they opened it up, the bag murmured, 'Yup!'
and it stretched and it gaped and it lurched.

And Ali looked on in amazement
as the bag seemed to billow and swell.
It gobbled the men and their weapons, and then
it golloped the horses as well.

it golloped the horses as well.

Then down on the pathway it settled
and shrank to original size.
'What a wonderful bag, not a wrinkle or sag!'
said Ali, while rubbing his eyes.

Eventually Ali felt hungry,
so he reached in the bag for a date.
He didn't suppose that the date was the nose
of the horrible robber – too late!

Young Ali, he pulled and he struggled,
and the robber plopped out on the ground.
He rose to full height. What a terrible sight,
as he lunged towards Ali and frowned,

'Young man, you are going to be mincemeat.
I'll chop you and fry you for tea . . .'
From the bag came a clink – that made the thug blink!
'Is that treasure? Hang on . . . let me see . . .'

He stuck his arm into the bag mouth
until he felt something to hold.
'I think that I've found something metal and round.
I'll bet that it's silver or gold.'

Out came the 'thing' as he pulled it . . .
Oh dear! The shield of a guard!
And there, on the end, oh, you guessed it,
my friend,
was the soldier himself, looking hard.

And out of the bag came his fellow,
and their weapons and horses as well.
The robber looked blighted. The guards looked delighted.
And one of them let out a yell!

'Look at this ruffian's finger!
We've done it. We've found it. Success!
He's wearing the ring of our great, mighty King.
So this is our robber. Oh yes!'

One of the guards turned to Ali.
'The King offered up a reward:
To the one who can bring back his favourite ring –
a bagful of gold from his hoard.'

Ali took hold of his djinn-bag,
to collect the reward that he'd won.
And the bag seemed to say, in a quizzical way,
'Together, now won't we have fun . . .?'

J ust as she finished her tale, Goat began to giggle.

"I was going to say it was funny," Monkey cut in. "But I don't think you should be laughing at your own story. Not before we do, anyway."

"No, no!" shrieked Goat. "There's something tickling me! All down my back. Oh, stop, stop! What is it?"

"It's me," squealed Spider crossly. "Your horns went right through my web, and I ended up running down your back to escape. I wish you'd look where you're going. It took me most of this morning to weave that web. And now it's ruined."

"Oooh! Ah . . . hoo, hoo!" screeched Goat. "I really am so . . . ooh, please stop tickling . . . so sorry! Oh, that's better."

Monkey had lifted Spider off Goat's back and was holding her in the palm of his hand.

"Now if you came along with us," he said with promise in his voice, "you would get to hear . . . The Tale of Tales!"

"Where?" said Spider doubtfully.

"Where we're going. Down in Volcano Valley," said Monkey, nodding keenly. "This afternoon," he added, to press the point home.

"And just how do you suppose I'd get there?" said Spider. "Being as I'm so small?"

"Why, you could weave a web between Goat's horns. That wouldn't tickle her. And you might catch some flies into the bargain, eh? You wouldn't mind that, Goat, would you?" said Monkey, looking directly at her.

"Not if Spider's got a good story to tell us," Goat replied. She said it almost like a challenge.

"A good story!" spluttered Spider. "Let me tell you that spiders have been the best weavers of yarns for years. Just take Spiderman Anansi. Think how many stories we have from him. And as a matter of fact he's my Great Uncle on my mother's side. Yes . . . I think I shall tell you all one of the famous Anansi stories. And if

you're not tickled by that, you won't be tickled by anything."

Goat agreed to have the web woven. "It'll deal with all those pesky flies that insist on buzzing round my face," she said agreeably.

So Monkey helped Spider string a thread from horn to horn over Goat's head. And soon, as the animals made their way along the Story Road, Spider was busy weaving a web and a tale all at the same time, such was her skill.

Anansi Meets Big Snake

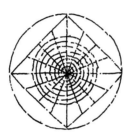

Anansi woke with a spidery yawn
and left his hole, to greet the dawn.

But waiting for him, just outside,
was a snake whose jaws lay open wide.

The snake just smiled and gave a hiss,
'Spider for breakfast. . . scrunchy – bliss!'

Anansi didn't gasp or blink.
There wasn't even time to think.

'Oh, Snake,' he warned, 'I have to say
a snake came by here yesterday.

'And he was big and mean and long,
with ripply muscles, really strong.

'He said that he was saving me
to eat this afternoon, for tea.

'So, eat me up and you're a thief,
and I guess that snake will give you grief.'

'Another snake as big as me?'
said Snake. 'Round here? Let me see!'

Anansi peered, 'You might be bigger. . .
I'd have to measure up your figure.'

And from the garden by his hole
Anansi picked a bamboo pole.

'Just stretch yourself from end to end.
I need you straight. Try not to bend.

'I'll tie your head here with this vine,
and now your tail. Good, that's fine.

'And now, to get your length just right,
I'll tie your middle nice and tight.'

Anansi scuttled back to take
a look at that enormous snake.

'Oh, yes,' he breathed. 'Gigantic. Phew!
I know no snake as big as you.

'The other snake was just a trick
to get you safely on that stick.

'But though you're big, you're not too shrewd.
I must be off now. See ya, dude!'

And so he scuttled on his way
to find some other tricks to play.

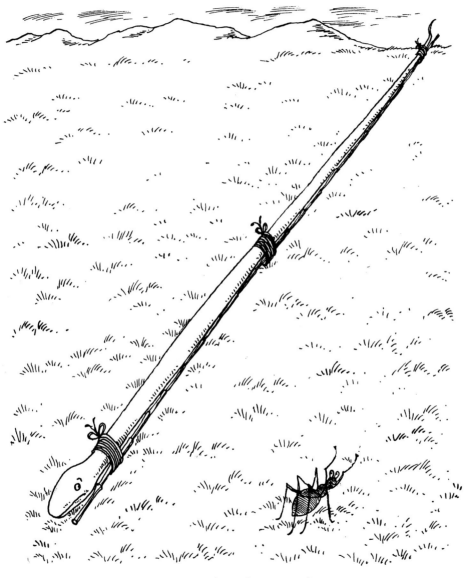

'I know no snake as big as you.'

"He sounds like a real character, your Great Uncle Anansi," said Elephant. "And not one to tangle with," he chuckled.

The others had all stopped and were listening hard. A great rumbling sound filled the air. What could it be? It seemed to be coming from the mouth of a large, dark cave beside the trail.

"I'm frightened," bleated Goat, edging nearer to Elephant for protection.

"Me too," said Monkey, getting ready to leap into the nearest branches at the first sign of danger.

"Are there ghosts or monsters around here?" asked Spider nervously. "It could be a troll or a demon, if it lives in a cave."

"Snoargh! Roargh! Sploargh!" came the awful sounds from the cave mouth. The animals huddled together with wide eyes fixed on the yawning, dark cavity. Except Elephant, who had his eyes narrowed and was pawing the ground with one foot, in readiness for a sudden attack from whatever lurked there in the shadows.

"Phloargh! Pshaw! Mmmummff . . . Hrrrummfff . . ."

All of a sudden, Elephant seemed to relax, then he threw back his head and laughed. Poor Monkey got such a shock he nearly tumbled off Elephant's neck and had to grab at his great flappy ears to keep his balance.

"It's Bear!" trumpeted Elephant so loudly that within moments a very grumpy Bear was stumbling out of the cave blinking and grunting.

"Don't do that," growled Bear when he'd managed to work out where he was and what was happening. "I was asleep and dreaming of nuts and berries. I need my rest. And it's so bad for my nerves to be woken with such a fright."

"This is no time for sleep," said Monkey. "Haven't you heard? Today is the day they're going to tell The Tale of Tales."

"Humph," growled Bear.

"Well, you can humph if you like," retorted Monkey. "But the rest of us are on our way to hear it. And if you've any sense at all you'll join us. Besides, we're telling stories along the way and it's turning out to be quite a party. But sleep if you like. We won't disturb you. Come on, friends. Let's leave Bear to his slumbers. Sleep well, old feller . . ."

As the animals all set off along the Story Road again it seemed that Bear had forgotten about snoozing, for he was lolloping along the track with them, suddenly wide awake.

"Now you mention it," he murmured thoughtfully, "there's a story I recall about one of the longest naps anyone ever took."

"That's the spirit," said Monkey. "Let's hear it, then."

So Bear began.

Rip Van Winkle

Rip Van Winkle, he lived in a cabin
with a cross-patch wife who was always jabbin'.

It was 'Rip, do this! and, Rip, do that!
and don't laze about like a sleepy old cat.'

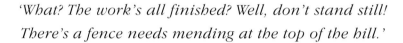

There was work in the cabin and work in the yard
and work in the fields, and it sure was hard.

'What? The work's all finished? Well, don't stand still!
There's a fence needs mending at the top of the hill.'

Well, Rip took the hammer and he walked up high.
When he got near the top, he stopped to sigh.

He looked at the view, breathed, 'Peace at last . . .'
Then he heard a little voice say, 'Dang and blast!'

Down by his feet was a tiny wee man,
saying, 'Help me, mister, if you can.'

The man had a barrel he was trying to roll
way up the track to a deep, dark hole.

And Rip, being friendly and kind and brave,
picked up the barrel and made for the cave.

He carried that barrel all the way down the hole.
When he got to the bottom, why, bless his soul!

The cave was crowded with tiny wee men.
Well, Rip just blinked, then he gawped once again.

The tiny wee man that Rip had helped
clambered on the barrel and waved and yelped,

'This here's Rip. He's an OK guy.
He carried my barrel from way up high.

'And though he's a human, I truly think
we should teach him to dance and give him a drink.'

Well, they found an old bucket and filled it up.
And to Rip, that bucket was the size of a cup.

And the beer was green, but it tasted great.
And they brought him crackers on a golden plate.

Then they got out a fiddle and a little banjo,
and they played him a tune with a ho, ho, ho!

He found he was dancing, and the boots on his feet
seemed to know the rhythm for they skipped to the beat.

But he soon got tired and he started to stoop,
and his heavy eyelids began to droop.

So he lay right down on the hard cave floor,
and his noisy nostrils started to snore.

Now, when he woke up he was stiff and cold,
and he felt a bit achy, as if he was old.

And the thing that was odd, yes, really weird:
his hair had gone white and he'd grown a long beard!

He went down the mountain and headed for his cabin,
with its things so neat and his wife so jabbin',

but when he got there, it was dark and dim,
and no cross wife came jabbin' at him.

The door swung wide and the stove was out,
and there wasn't a soul to be seen about.

There was dust on the floor and cracks in the panes.
There were thick, grey cobwebs choking the drains.

And as he stood gawping and scratching his head,
a man came by, saying 'Gone and dead . . .

his hair had gone white and he'd grown a long beard!

'Widow Van Winkle died long ago.
And her husband, Rip, . . don't nobody know.

'He went up the hill on a fine summer's day.
Some say the goblins took him away.

'Whatever did happen, he never came back
to his jabbin' old wife and his neat little shack.'

Well, Rip just looked, then he turned his back
on the tumbledown cottage, and he took the track.

He didn't say a word. He was dazed and dumb.
And he stumbled right back the way he'd come.

He found that cave so dark and deep
and he lay straight down and went back to sleep.

And some folk say he's sleeping still,
deep in the heart of Dreaming Hill.

"Well," said Spider. "I hope I never sleep like that. And I don't think my web would last long enough, anyway."

"Help!" cried a tiny voice. "Look out. Don't tread on me!"

Elephant had stopped with one foot frozen in mid-air. He reached down under that foot with the tip of his trunk and brought out a tiny, pink, wriggling worm.

"Oh, I'm so sorry!" blushed Worm. "I shouldn't have been there. It's so dangerous to cross

the trail in daylight. Especially at my speed."

"You're safe now," crooned Elephant. And he lifted her up on to the tip of one of Goat's horns where Spider could keep her company.

"And you're lucky too," said Monkey. "Because we're getting together a gang to go and hear The Tale of Tales, down in Volcano Valley. And we're taking it in turns to tell stories on the

way. So you're just in time to tell yours if you stick with us."

But at the thought of telling a story to the entire company, Worm got into a fluster.

"Oh, I couldn't tell a whole story by myself. I mean, I think I know some stories, but I really couldn't tell one properly on my own. I don't think I could manage that."

"Have a shot," said Spider. "You never know what you can do until you've tried. I'm sure you could come up with something if you stretched yourself," she chuckled naughtily.

"Yes, go on," urged Goat. "We won't make fun of you. We'll just listen, and help sort you out if you get yourself tied in a knot," she giggled.

"Well," said Worm, blushing and taking a deep breath. "Here goes . . ."

And as the animals went trotting off down the Story Road, Worm curled around the tip of Goat's horn and did her best to squeeze out a tale that held together.

Worm's Tale

Once upon a time,
now, let me see . . .
there were two brothers,
or was it three?
But wasn't it sisters . . .?
Hmmm . . . maybe . . .
brothers or sisters –
I don't know.
On with the story,
here we go:

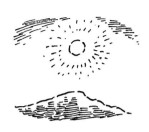

Well, as they tell it,
one fine day . . .
or was it night-time?
Can't quite say . . .
Anyhow, whether
by sun or moon,
they took a boat,
or an air balloon . . .?
However it was,
they got there soon.

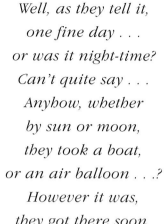

Where did they get to?
Can't recall.
A castle? A cavern?
A towering wall?
Whatever it was
was under a spell.
What was the matter?
They couldn't tell.
And I can't remember,
either way.

But, as it happened,
so they say,
they trapped the witch
(or was it a troll?)
up in a tower
or down a hole.
And they took the treasure
and all got rich . . .
no, didn't they drop it
in the ditch?
Or was it the troll
they pushed in there?
And if they did, well,
was that fair?
And was it honest?
Do we care?

up in a tower or down a hole.

But I'm sure they freed
a young princess
who was fast asleep,
or in distress?
Hmmm, I think they did . . .
oh, yes!
And then they asked her
back for tea –
and that will have to do,
from me.
This tale has writhed me
round the bend,
so this had better be
the end.
But which end's which,
and where's the middle,
well, sorting that
will be a fiddle.
I'll pass the problem
on to you.
I think that's it
from me now – Phew!"

As Worm finished her tale with great relief, the others praised her for her effort. They knew she'd tried hard and didn't want to hurt her feelings. So out they came with congratulations.

"Jolly good."

"Well done."

"Nice try."

"Bravo!"

And while these kind murmurs were going on, they came across a dog digging busily. He seemed to be on his fourth hole and he was beginning to show signs of despair.

"What's up friend?" said Elephant.

"Lost a bone," Dog panted. "Can't find it anywhere. I'm sure I buried it just around here."

"Leave it," cried Monkey. "Come along with us."

"What, and leave a good marrow bone in the ground?" gasped Dog. "You must be joking!"

"Bones," said Monkey wisely, "can be had again and again. But today we are going to hear The Tale of Tales. How often does a chance like that come up? And besides, your bone will be safe there

in the ground till you return. Why, you can hardly find it yourself, it's so well hidden."

"I suppose so," sighed Dog. "Well then, I'll join you. I could do with some company to cheer me up."

"And we could do with a story to cheer us up," bleated Goat. "Come on, Dog, you must have heard of stories, lying around the fireside in cottages as dogs do. A tail to wag and a tale to tell, that's the way with dogs, eh, don't they say?"

So Dog took his turn and dipped into his store of stories. As the growing gang of animals made their way along the Story Road, he told them a stirring tale of loyalty and courage, just as you might expect of a trusty dog.

The Hobyas

In a neat little cottage, by the edge of a wood,
lived a little old couple as best they could.
They thatched their roof and it kept out the storm,
and they fed their fire and it kept them warm.

Their little dog Turpy watched at night
with his cross little bark and his brave little bite.
He wouldn't ask who, or why, or how.
He'd throw back his head with a bow, wow, wow!

They all lived happily till one dark day
the horrible hobyas came that way.
They hid in the wood till down went the sun,
then out from the trees they came at a run.

And as they came, the night breeze rang
with a mean little song that the hobyas sang:
'Out come the hobyas, skip, skip, skip,
with teeth that bite and nails that nip.

'Nasty little hobyas, tripping through the night,
with wicked little eyes and teeth that bite.
The hobya tummies are hungry – ooh!
We're on our way and we might eat you!'

Little dog Turpy heard their song.
His bark came loud and brave and strong.
The hobyas stopped, and back they ran,
but up from his bed got the little old man.

'Little dog Turpy, what's this fuss?
There's no-one here but you and us.
A dog mustn't bark at nothing at all.'
And he tied poor Turpy up to the wall.

'Here come the hobyas, skip, skip, skip,'

He went off to bed with a grump and a frown,
as little dog Turpy settled back down.
Then out from the woods so spooky and black,
the horrible hobyas skipped straight back.

And as they skipped, the night breeze rang
with the horrible song the hobyas sang:

'Here come the hobyas, skip, skip, skip,
on a horrible hobya hunting trip.
We're hungry now for a hobya feed.
Our sharp little teeth will make you bleed.'

Little dog Turpy heard their song.
His bark came loud and brave and strong.
The hobyas turned, and off they ran,
but back from his bed stumped the little old man.

'Little dog Turpy, what's this fuss?
There's no-one here but you and us.
You're waking us up while the night's still dark.
I'll muzzle you up, so you can't bark.'

He went off to bed with a grump and a frown,
as little dog Turpy settled back down.
Then out came the hobyas, skip, skip, skip,
with their teeth that bite and their nails that nip.

Poor old Turpy was muzzled and tied,
so he just couldn't bark, however he tried.
The hobyas sneaked through the creaky door
and they tiptoed over the cottage floor.

They tumbled the woman right into a sack,
and carried her shrieking, quickly back.
'We are the hobyas, hee-hee-hee.
We've a nice, plump woman to eat for tea.'

'Stop!' cried the old man. 'Turpy! Help!'
But tied-up Turpy could hardly yelp.
'Oh!' groaned the man. 'I'm such a dope!'
And he took off the muzzle and cut the rope.

Off ran Turpy, up to the wood,
and the old man followed, as best he could.
Turpy sniffed and snuffed, and then
he found where the hobyas had their den.

They'd hung the sack right up in their store,
and off they'd gone to look for more.
The old man heard his poor wife shout,
so he opened the sack and let her out.

That brave dog Turpy jumped inside,
and they hung the sack, then went to hide.
For, as they listened, the night breeze rang
with the horrible song the hobyas sang:

'The dog, the man, have both run off,
and there's no-one left down here to scoff.
But we stole that little old wife tonight,
so we'll eat her slowly bite by bite.'

The hobyas soon came skipping back,
and they went to find their midnight snack.
They reached their sack down off the hook,
and they opened it up to take a look.

Out jumped Turpy, quick as a flash,
with a snip-snap snarl and a bite and a gnash.

80

He gobbled those hobyas, one by one,
then he growled to say that the job was done.

Then home went the couple with little dog Turpy.
He felt proud – but a little bit burpy!
(Horrible hobyas, fresh from the wood,
probably just don't taste too good.)

'Good dog, Turpy,' the old folk said.
'From now we'll both sleep safe in bed.
No more muzzle and no more rope.
And no more hobyas – so we hope!'

"Not bad," said a strange voice quietly, "for a dog." The animals all turned to where Cat was padding along to one side of them.

"Where did you spring from?" gibbered Monkey. "You gave me

a shock, you did, just appearing like that."

"I'd have smelled her," growled Dog, "if I hadn't been so busy with my story."

Cat gave Dog an uneasy sideways look. "Well, am I welcome here or not?" she mewed, glancing round at the others.

"Of course you're welcome," boomed Elephant. "We're off on a journey together . . ."

"To hear The Tale of Tales," Monkey cut in, wanting it to be known that this was his idea.

"It can't be far now," said Bear. "It's going to be in Volcano Valley, and I can already feel the ground rumbling from here."

"That's your tummy," said Spider cheekily.

"Or Elephant's breathing," added Worm.

"And we're all telling tales along the way," continued Monkey eagerly, "to pass the time and to make the whole thing more fun.

"Dark is so much more fun, don't you think?"

So you can join us and take your turn now, if you like."

"Well, thank you, I will," mewed Cat demurely. "And, as it happens, I could tell you another tale that occurs mostly in the dark," she purred. "Dark is so much more fun, don't you think?"

And for a moment her eyes flashed green. No-one interrupted her, so she started right in. But not before Dog had moved as far away from her as he could, without straying out of earshot.

Jack and The Bush

Jack lay sprawling late in bed,
when in came Ma. 'Oh, Jack,' she said,

'The oats and peas and beans won't grow,
and what we'll do I just don't know.

'The sack of potatoes is all used up.
There's no more milk for jug or cup.

'Old Nell our cow's completely dry.
I think we'll starve. Oh me, oh my!

'It's market day. So take Old Nell.
She's all we've left to try and sell.

'Get what you can for her, dear Jack.
Then buy some things and bring them back:

'Some bread and butter, some sugar and tea,
and choose a length of cloth for me.

'This dress of mine is old and worn.
It's all in tatters, patched and torn.

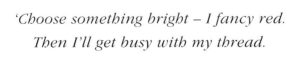

'Choose something bright – I fancy red.
Then I'll get busy with my thread.

'And if Old Nell brings in enough,
please try to get some other stuff:

'Some flour, some eggs, some apples – ripe,
and p'raps some baccy for my pipe,

'a drop of whisky, nice and strong.
Now, off you go, Jack. Don't be long.'

Young Jack got up and took Old Nell.
And, sure, the market day went well.

The price she fetched was fifteen pounds,
so Jack went off and did his rounds.

He managed all his mother's list.
There wasn't one thing that he missed.

The cloth he found was red and bright.
It looked and felt exactly right.

Then, feeling he could use some grub,
he dropped by at the local pub.

He drank a pint, or maybe two.
And then, I fear, another few.

So, off he toddled, feeling warm.
But, as he went, there came a storm.

The rain it lashed. The wind it blew.
And soon the moon went out of view.

But, though the way was hid from sight,
young Jack could walk it day or night.

He whistled as he went along,
then hummed a tune and sang a song.

Not far from home he passed a bush.
Its branches squeaked. The wind went whoosh.

Its branches made a creaky croak,
as if a poor old woman spoke.

Its shape was like a bent old hag,
so Jack reached down inside his bag.

'Now, come on, Granny. Take a sip.
This whisky here will wet your lip.

'The weather's rough. It isn't right.
You shouldn't be out here at night.'

The bush, of course, could not reply,
so Jack reached out. He thought he'd try

to coax her to his cosy croft
and make a bed for her, all soft.

But, deary me, the bush was thorny,
and, like a hag's hands, old and scrawny.

It scratched his arms and made him bleed
and put Jack off his kind good deed.

'Well, stay here if you must, old girl.
But round about you I will curl

'this length of cloth so fine and bright,
to keep you warm this stormy night.'

Then Jack went home and fell in bed,
and in the morning woke and said,

'Now daylight's here, I'll take the path
and help old Granny to our hearth.

'She's sure to want a cup of tea.
Ah, that will make her come with me.'

But in the pallid light of dawn
Jack saw the creaky, ragged thorn.
And – oh! the cloth was ripped and torn.

Jack saw the blunder that he'd made.
He stomped back home and fetched a spade.

Then, with a loud and angry shout,
he dug the bush completely out.

'That length of cloth was for my mother.
I'll see that you won't ruin another!'

He dug its roots out from the ground,
but then, beneath them, there he found

an ancient box, a secret stash,
a-brim with gold and jewels and cash!

His mother, puffing up to see,
caught sight of it and cried, 'Whoopee!

'This treasure's just the thing we need.
We're saved! Oh, now we're rich indeed.

an ancient box, a secret stash, a-brim with gold and jewels and cash!

'But what are you up to now, dear Jack?'
'Ma, I'm putting this thorn bush back.

'The bush has made us really rich.
I can't just dump it in the ditch.

'I'll bed its roots back in the earth,
then water them for all I'm worth.'

That plant soon grew back, bright and strong,
while Jack and Ma's life rolled along.

Night led to day, and day to night,
and Jack and Ma were both alright.

"Oh, yes," barked Dog. "I loved the digging up bit, where the treasure was in the roots of the bush. Just like finding a great hoard of bones!" Then he remembered himself. "Quite good . . . erh, for a cat, I suppose . . ."

But the animals were now arriving at a place where the trail split into two.

"Which way?" murmured Monkey.

"Indeed . . ." echoed Elephant, scratching his head with the tip of his trunk.

"To where?" hooted a voice above them. It was Owl.

"To Volcano Valley, of course," said Monkey, looking up to where Owl sat blinking on a branch. "To hear The Tale of Tales."

"Either way," said Owl. "They join up again at the other end of the lake. And then

the trail leads along to the valley. It's not far now. I'll show you. And I'll tell you a story of my own as we go."

So Owl fluttered down to settle on Elephant's head, in front of Monkey. And as the company chose the left-hand route, which seemed more curious and interesting, Owl entertained them all with a spooky story from long ago.

The Piper and The Pookah

There was a poor piper lived under a hill.
If he's not gone away, then he's living there still.
And only one tune could that poor piper play.
But he blew it his best both by night and by day.

Returning one night from a frolicsome feast,
he was joined on the road by a lumbering beast.
He knew it at once for the cumbersome Pookah,
with a head like a horse, and a terrible spooker.

Now, Pookahs were famous, but Pookahs were few,
and you never could tell what a Pookah might do.
But although the poor piper was trembling with fright,
he greeted the Pookah with, 'Top of the night!'

The Pookah put piper and pipe on his back
and he took them a journey along the dark track.
'Now play us a tune,' boomed the Pookah at last.
So the terrified piper attempted a blast.

And, although there was only one tune that he knew,
to the piper's amazement, right there as he blew,
his fingers they tingled, his head seemed to thrill,
as all manner of tunes tumbled out, played with skill.

Said the Pookah, 'We'll go to the top of the hill
where a gaggle of hags have been eating their fill.
They've passed round the potcheen and had a good swig,
and they're wanting to lift up their legs in a jig.'

So up went the Pookah, the piper and all,
and they piped out the tunes for the haggardy ball.
He was paid for his pains from a coffer of gold –
as much as his hat and his pockets might hold.

The Pookah returned him safe back to his cot.
But when he awoke in the dawn, what he'd got
was a hat and both pockets not brimming with gold,
but crackling with leaves that were crumbling and old.

'I'm a poor man as ever,' he sighed. ' 'Tis a pity.'
And he pulled out his pipe just to play his old ditty.
But there as he fingered and blew, to his thrill,
he discovered the Pookah had left him the skill.

And ever since then, though he hasn't the gold,
he has all the tunes that a piper can hold.
He carries his pipe and he plays it with pride.
So, if he's a poor man, well, you can decide.

and they piped out the tunes for the haggardy ball.

As Owl finished her story, the company were approaching the far tip of the lake.

"There's a lovely pool here," she said. "Just perfect for bathing. You all look as if you could do with freshening up."

The animals looked at one another. It was true. They were very dusty. So in they all went, splashing and squirting and sporting, and then just lolling about in the sparkly water, as all of the dust of the Story Road washed off them. And there they all lay, until they felt ready to move on.

"Come on," said Owl. "It's nearly time now."

And as they waded up out of the lake they felt refreshed and ready for something new. So they shook off the droplets, leaving the late afternoon sun to finish drying them. Then they all made their way down into Volcano Valley. And what a crowd they found there!

The prattling parrots had not managed to keep it all to themselves. Being parrots, they'd kept repeating it here and there, until all of nature's creation knew about 'The Tale of Tales.' Almost every kind of creature seemed to have come. There were timid little mice and shrews, and great big buffalo and bison.

There were worms, centipedes, ants and earwigs, and there was every imaginable kind of bird. There were domestic dogs and cats and pigs, and there were wild, ferocious tigers, panthers, lions and pumas. There were cuddly little koala bears and tall, elegant giraffes. Think of an animal, and you'd probably see at least one there. Iguana? Yes. Gnu? Of course. Except perhaps for fish.

But no, even a few of those had managed it, for they sat in the nearby stream with their mouths and eyes out of the water, hoping to catch some part of the

Great Tale that had been rumoured.

Monkey's company were just about the last to arrive, save for a few other stragglers arriving in dribs and drabs.

"I knew it," he almost shrieked with glee as they saw the vast crowd. "I was right. It was worth it!"

It looked like the story was to be told from the mouth of Hot Air Cave, a kind of grotto which stood at the base of the volcano. But who was to tell the story? This was still a mystery. There was an air of excitement as the friends found a spare patch of ground to sit down on. As they watched and waited, an ancient baboon stood up to face the crowd from the cave mouth. He thumped his staff upon the rocky floor to call for silence.

And there, down in Volcano Valley, as the sun set quietly behind the surrounding hills, the ancient baboon lit a fire to light the cave mouth, and all of the animals waited for the appearance of the storyteller who would at last tell to them this Tale of Tales.

Gradually a deep silence settled over the whole valley. The crowd sat very still till all that could be heard was the faint crackling of the flames at the cave mouth. Then, from within the cave, a clear, deep voice began to issue. Who the Teller was,

the ancient baboon lit a fire to light the cave mouth

no-one could make out. But the cave itself worked like a natural megaphone, so that every word could be heard distinctly right across the whole valley.

And so, as they all sat hushed and listening, there where the Story Road ended, The Tale of Tales began with those magical, well-worn words . . .

"Once upon a time . . ."

Some other David Fickling books that work like magic:

Once Upon a Tide
by Tony Mitton and Selina Young

Riddledy Piggledy
by Tony Mitton and Paddy Mounter

Handbag Friends
by Sally Lloyd-Jones and Sue Heap

Ahoyty Toyty
by Helen Stephens

Poochie-Poo
by Helen Stephens